A Piece of Cake

with a Sprinkle of Kindness

By

Leydi Arias

Dedication

I dedicate this book to my mother; thank you for your unconditional love and support throughout every life achievement.

Acknowledgments

I would like to thank the Children at The Willows Ay 2022/23. For being the first group to portray the idea of "lunch dates."

It is 7:00 am in the morning! Time to get ready for school. This is how I get ready.

1. First thing, I must brush my teeth.

 My mom combs my hair.

4. I eat breakfast.

 I play for a little.

6. I get everything ready in my backpack.

7. I get in the car, and off we go to school.

As soon as I get to school, I run to go find Ashely. She is my favorite friend to play with at school.

I love playing with Ashely in the sand Area.
Building castles or pretending to build
volcanos.

Ashely is my favorite friend. I can play with her all day and never get bored. Sometimes I forget to play with my other friends at school because I get so busy playing with Ashely.

But in my school, we do something special
called Lunch Dates. This helps me get to
know other friends and reminds me that
there are other great friends that I can
play with.

So, this is how lunch dates work at my school. Before we go to lunch or we wash our hands, we sit down in circle time with all my classmates.

My teacher calls on a student, and that person has to choose someone that they normally don't play much with. Once you pick that friend, we go wash our hands and sit together.

Even Though sometimes I feel sad because I don't get to have a Lunch date with Ashely. That is okay because we sit in the same room space for lunch, and that is what matters.

For example, today, my lunch date was Erick. When we opened our lunch box, we both had pizza. I learned that Erick loves pizza, his favorite animals are dinosaurs, and he loves the color yellow like me and Ashely.

After lunch, I invited Erick to play with me and Ashely. Now, we are three friends playing together. I love doing lunch dates at my school.

Because it reminds me that there is more than one friend that I can play with. I love sharing a piece of kindness with everyone.

It's an easy gesture to do. It's like a piece of cake with a sprinkle of kindness.